Large Print fo

tell me a

HANUMAN

MW00973206

ANURAG MEHTA

Nita Mehta
Publications
Enriching Young Minds

Birth of Hanuman

Once, Punjikasthala, an Apsara (celestial beauty) was annoying a sage with her inappropriate behaviour.

"I curse you! For this disobedience, you will live on earth now. You will be called Anjana and will take the form of a monkey." As the sage's curse hit her, a horrified Punjikasthala was hurtled down to earth, where she landed into the forests of the monkey world.

Feeling sorry for herself, Anjana sadly wandered through the forest and soon lay down on a grassy hill under a shady tree. The breeze pleasantly wafted over her and she fell asleep. Anjana did not know the breeze caressing her was actually Lord Vayu, the God of Wind.

His divinity allowed him to look deep into Anjana's mind and know her tragic story. When Anjana awoke, she was swept into a whirl of loving attention from Lord Vayu. "Who is that?" she said.

"I am Vayu, the God of Wind. I have fallen in love with you and want to give you a son."

Thereafter, a son was born to Anjana and when she saw him she felt he was the most beautiful being in the universe, even though he was a monkey.

Vayu was very happy on seeing her joy. He circled round the exultant pair three times and blessed them, saying, "Your baby will be called Hanuman, son of the wind.

As my son, he will have my strength, my speed and my power to fly through the world. He will be kind, brave and mighty and will do much good in the world. Be proud of him!"

Thus, Anjana gave birth to the magnificent Monkey-God who became renowned as Hanuman.

The Gods witnessing the birth of this extraordinary child knew his life would be an exciting one.

Hanuman's Childhood

One bright sunny day, Anjana went for a walk along with young Hanuman.

"Mother, look!" little Hanuman pointed his tiny fingers towards the sun. Anjana smiled indulgently and looked up too. "Mother," Hanuman lisped, "What is that round, shining thing?"

"That is the sun," answered his mother. Hanuman gazed up. His small face shifted side to side in curiosity. Little Hanuman thought that the twinkling brightness of the round, blazing object needed to be inspected. With an agile spring, Hanuman reached out and tried to grab the sun. Seeing this, the sun jumped and warned,

"Hey...stay away...whaaa....!" But Hanuman had grasped him firmly in his little hands.

"Ow...let go, let go, yeow! What is the meaning of this?" the sun bawled helplessly. Hanuman inquisitively rolled the sun around his tiny fingers. The sun's face cringed and cawed at this intrusion. But Hanuman was not letting go. With a breathy giggle, he chortled, "This is a ball, mother." Before Anjana could stop him, Hanuman began to dribble the sun like a ball! The sun groaned and winced in pain.

"Uhhhhhhh-ouch-ow akkkk!! Help! Somebody help me!" shuddered the bouncing sun.

"Oh, this is so much fun!" Hanuman gurgled, ignoring the sun's discomfort.

"Lord Indra, keeper of the sky, save me from this monkey boy," cried the wretched sun.

Whooooosh! The sky thundered in response to an arrival. Yes, the arrival was that of the Sky God, Indra, who rode his elephant Airawat. Sigh! Hanuman ignored the God of thunder and lightening and continued to play with his sun ball.

Hanuman was having such an enjoyable time that he refused to listen. Indra got off from his elephant and tried to stop Hanuman. But he was unable to do so. If Indra came one way, Hanuman dribbled the other way. Indra huffed and puffed across the skies, failing desperately at his attempt.

Frustrated, Indra's anger spilled over into dark ominous clouds. Angry growls rumbled across the heavens.

Indra reached out to his quiver full of thunderbolts and picked one. "Hark! I throw this Vajra (divine weapon) at you. Beware of its effects!" he bellowed dramatically.

With one strong swift motion, Indra threw the bolt towards Hanuman. The weapon struck its target!

Little Hanuman fell down unconscious. Anjana was horrified. She cried out Hanuman's name desperately, trying to revive him. The sun vaulted back to its place and Indra left, having saved the sun. Somewhere else, an inner feeling, that his son needed him, disturbed Lord Vayu. With a rush of air, he curved towards the valley of flowers.

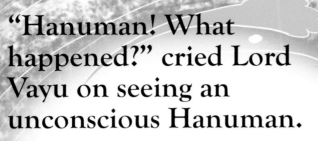

"Hanuman! What happened?" cried Lord Vayu on seeing an unconscious Hanuman.

Anjana continued sobbing not answering Vayu.

Lord Vayu blustered a current of air, bawling, "Tell me who did this to little Hanuman?"

Getting no answers, the incensed Vayu swooped up his son and revolved around outer space. "I will take the air from the three worlds with me. Air will only return when Hanuman breathes again!"

Vayu taking away all the air from the world left the plants, animals and people gasping.

"Forgive us! Give us air or else we will die," they choked at Vayu to relent from his curse.

But Lord Vayu was so infuriated that he refused to budge. As there was no air, all living things began to wither.

When Indra got to know about the consequence of his action, he repented.

"What have I done? That was Lord Vayu's son! My anger has caused this mess."

Lord Indra reproached himself.

"I shall apologize to Lord Vayu," decided Indra.

15

Lord Indra along with the other Gods reached Lord Vayu. Respectfully, they apologized to him. Furthermore, with the divine powers vested in them, they revived Hanuman. In addition, they blessed Hanuman with untold powers and immortality.

"His body will be as strong as thunder while his mind will be as sharp as lightening. He will live longer than any creature in the cosmos.

Fire will not harm him, temptations will not distract him. He will therefore be known as Vajranga-bali," said the Gods.

Pleased with these boons, Vayu released air back into the cosmos.

17

Hanuman Chooses His Guru

Hanuman decided to educate himself and chose Surya as his guru. "You see everything there is to see in the universe and you possess all knowledge. Please accept me as your pupil," he requested the Sun-God.

The Sun-God accepted him as his pupil. Hanuman flew before the solar chariot withstanding the glare until he became well versed with the great knowledge that Surya imparted on him.

In time, Hanuman became a master of literature, grammar, politics, commerce, economics, music, the arts, the sciences, philosophy, even mysticism and the occult.

After completing his education, it was time to pay his fee.

"Watching you study was payment enough," said Surya. But Hanuman insisted that he wished to give something to express his gratitude. The Sun-God said, "Please look after the welfare of my son, Sugriva."

"So be it," said Hanuman and made his way to Kishkinda, the land of the monkeys.

Kishkinda was a dense forest ruled by the monkey king, Vali.

Sugriva was Vali's younger brother. As a result of a mis-understanding, Vali had become Sugriva's enemy and had sworn to kill him.

Hanuman gave protection to Sugriva against Vali. Sugriva and Hanuman made Mount Rishyamukha their home. Sugriva never went out as he was scared that Vali would harm him. He relied on Hanuman to bring him news of the outside world.

One day, Sugriva and Hanuman saw a chariot flying over Mount Rishyamukha, moving in the South direction. They heard a woman's cry and a man's laugh and noticed that the woman in the aerial chariot was casting off her ornaments, as if to mark a trail.

A few days later, Hanuman saw two strangers on the banks of the river Pampa. They were young men, one dark and one fair. There was a regal air about them. But they were dressed like hermits with clothes of bark and matted hair. Both looked sad. On enquiring, Hanuman got to know that they were the princes of Ayodhya, Rama and Lakshmana.

Hanuman introduced himself and invited the two brothers to Sugriva's abode.

As they looked too tired to climb the hill, he increased his size, picked them up, placed them on his shoulders and flew to Mount Rishyamukha.

On the way, he told them, all about Sugriva and his enemity with Vali.

Hanuman and Sugriva told Rama that they had seen a chariot flying over Rishyamukha carrying a man and woman. Hanuman brought out the ornaments the monkeys had collected from the forest floor.

"These are Sita's ornaments," said Rama, teary eyed.

Rama asked Sugriva if he knew where Ravana lives.

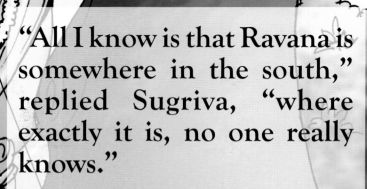

"All I know is that Ravana is somewhere in the south," replied Sugriva, "where exactly it is, no one really knows."

Hanuman brokered a deal between Sugriva and Rama.

Rama would help Sugriva overthrow Vali and Sugriva would in turn help Rama rescue Sita. Instructed by Rama, Sugriva went to Kishkinda and challenged Vali to a fight. Rama, meanwhile, hid in the bushes, waiting for an opportune moment to kill Vali with his arrow. Sugriva wore a garland of flowers round his neck so that he could be distinguished from his brother. While they were engaged in battle, Rama shot an arrow straight through Vali's heart which killed him instantly. Sugriva was crowned the king of Kishkinda.

Now it was Surgriva's turn to fulfill his promise. Soon they discovered that Sita was in Lanka. Lanka was a thousand miles away and the sea in between was rough and full of serpents and monsters.

The monkeys wondered how they could make their way to Lanka over a thousand miles of sea. "It is too far to swim," said one. "And the sea is too rough to sail," said another.

"We should ask Hanuman to leap across," suggested Jambuvan, the bear.

As Hanuman mustered the strength, his body began to grow in size, expanding to enormous proportions.

His face glowed like the rising sun and energy throbbed through his powerful limbs.

Hanuman climbed to the peak of Mount Mahendra that stood overlooking the southern sea. Shouting, "Victory to Lord Rama," he sprang to the sky and the impulse of his leap flattened the mountain.

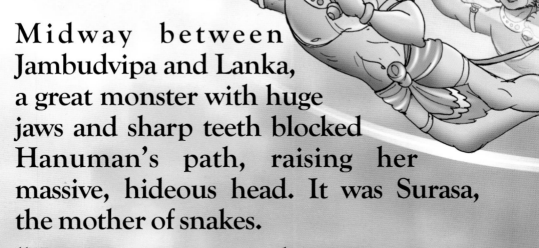

Midway between Jambudvipa and Lanka, a great monster with huge jaws and sharp teeth blocked Hanuman's path, raising her massive, hideous head. It was Surasa, the mother of snakes.

"You cannot go on unless you enter my mouth and if you get in, you'll never get out," she cackled as she opened her mouth.

The upper jaw touched the sky and the lower lay beneath the crested waves.

Realizing he could not bypass Surasa, Hanuman increased his size to make it difficult for Surasa to swallow him.

Surasa, however, widened her jaws to accommodate the flying monkey. Hanuman kept growing bigger and bigger and Surasa's mouth kept getting wider and wider. Then, Hanuman reduced his size to that of a mosquito, zoomed into Surasa's mouth and before she could shut her mouth, he was out; all in a blink of an eye.

"There I have entered your mouth. Now let me pass," he said. "Very clever," said an impressed Surasa and disappeared into the blue sea to let Hanuman go.

Hanuman Reaches Lanka

At long last, having crossed a thousand miles of sea, Hanuman saw the island of Trikuta on the horizon. Above was the sapphire blue sky. Below was the emerald green sea. In between stood a grand citadel of gold with bright red banners fluttering atop every tower. It was Lanka!

Vishwakarma, the architect of the Gods, had built this city to befit the grandeur of the yaksha-king Kubera, its original ruler. Moulded out of gold, it was more beautiful than Amravati, the abode of the Gods.

The sheer splendour of Ravana's city left Hanuman speechless.

'If this city is so beautiful from the outside, what would it be like on the inside?' wondered Hanuman.

When Hanuman reached Lanka, it was midnight. All the rakshasas were asleep. except Lankini, who stomped outside the walls of Lanka.

She never slept. Lankini was a warrior-maiden who had blazing eyes and mighty arms bearing weapons of every kind. She blocked Hanuman's entry into Ravana's city. "Identify yourself," she said. Impatient to pass through the gates, Hanuman revealed his gigantic form. His head reached the celestial realms, his feet stretched into the nether regions. His tail lashed the sea to whip up a storm and his eyes flashed thunder. He breathed out fire and let out a piercing war cry. A terrified Lankini ran away, leaving Lanka unguarded.

Under the cover of darkness, Hanuman entered Lanka, reducing himself to the size of a bee so that he could fly unnoticed through the city of rakshasas.

Finally after some time, Hanuman entered a pleasure-garden located at the far end of Ravana's palace. There, under an Ashoka tree, he found a woman looking forlorn. A large number of demonesses watched over her.

Hanuman scrambled up a tree and secretly watched her. The woman was crying, whispering Rama's name.

Hanuman realized that he had stumbled upon Sita. At that moment, King Ravana himself entered. Hanuman choked with anger but stayed hidden. Ravana glared at the sobbing Sita and barked, "I have waited enough. Be sensible and become my queen."

At his arrogant words, Sita's chin rose and she said firmly, "Go away! My Lord Rama will come and you will be punished!"

Ravana spluttered and spat with fury, "Rama cannot cross the ocean! Forget about him." Saying that, he stomped out.

After Ravana had departed, Hanuman decided it was time to present himself. When the demonesses guarding Sita fell asleep, Hanuman dropped Rama's ring before Sita, arousing her curiosity. When she looked up, she saw a monkey saluting her.

"I am Hanuman, son of Vayu, Sugriva's minister and Rama's messenger," he said.

"Oh! My Lord has sent a message!" Sita said excitedly with tears of joy in her eyes. Hanuman informed her in great detail about all that had happened since her abduction. He suddenly had a bright idea.

Sita shook her head and said softly, "No! Tell my Lord that I will wait for him to come here and vanquish this evil demon. Let him take me back home with honour." Hanuman agreed, marveling at Sita's dignity and wisdom.

"I shall tell him of your desire. Before I go, kindly give me something as a proof of our meeting."

Sita gave Hanuman her jewel-studded hairpin. His mission complete, Hanuman prepared to leave Lanka. But he did not want to go without teaching Ravana a lesson or two.

He decided to vandalize the pleasure-garden where Sita was being held prisoner. He leapt from tree to tree, squashing the flowers and crushing the fruits. The royal guards were summoned, but were no match for the mighty Monkey God. When news of the vandalism reached Ravana, he dispatched his young son Akshaya to capture the miscreant. Eager to prove his valour, the young prince entered the garden in his chariot and shot an arrow at Hanuman. Hanuman, in turn, hurled a rock and smashed Akshaya's skull.

Hanuman is Captured

The death of Akshaya at the hands of a monkey alarmed Ravana who sent Meghanath, his eldest son, to capture the trouble maker. Meghanath was the most powerful warrior in Lanka with many victories to his credit. He had even defeated Indra in battle, earning the title of Indrajit, vanquisher of the king of the Gods.

Indrajit soon discovered that the monkey in the garden was no ordinary beast. Exasperated, he was forced to raise his bow and shoot arrows at the monkey. But Hanuman simply caught the arrows and broke them.

Indrajit finally shot the Brahmastra, an arrow reverberating with the power of Brahma. The arrow had the power to kill a God but it only stunned Hanuman. When Hanuman fell down, Indrajit bound him with nagapasha, self-coiling magical serpent-ropes, and dragged him into Ravana's court.

All the residents of Lanka gathered in Ravana's court to see the monkey who had killed Akshaya and confounded Indrajit. When Hanuman introduced himself as the messenger of Rama, Ravana angrily shouted, "You are only a monkey, not a messenger."

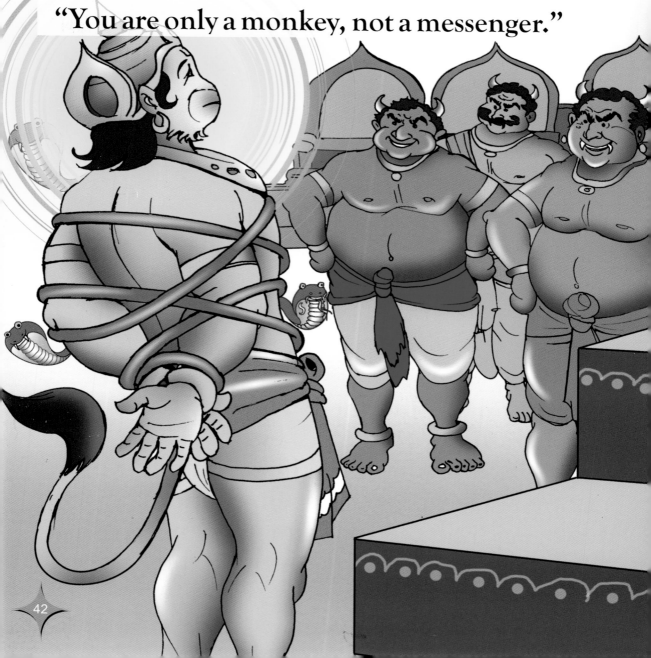

Ravana and the whole court burst out laughing. Only Vibhishana did not laugh.

Vibhishana was Ravana's younger brother who had repeatedly counseled against the abduction of Rama's wife.

"Brother, let us hear what this monkey has to say," pleaded Vibhishana.

"Be quiet or leave, Vibhishana," yelled Ravana.

The courtiers stifled a giggle. Humiliated, Vibhishana bowed his head and left the court.

"Well, untie these ropes and offer me a seat. Don't you rakshasas know how to extend courtesy that is due to a messenger," said Hanuman.

"A cage in the royal zoo will suit you better," said Indrajit.

Ravana and all the rakshasas roared in laughter.

Hanuman was not amused. Since he was not offered a seat, he decided to make a seat for himself.

First, he puffed his chest and split the nagapasha that bound him. Then, he lengthened his tail, coiled it around to make a tower, leapt on it and sat down looking down upon Ravana.

"A seat higher than Ravana's throne befits Rama's messenger," he said much to Ravana's irritation.

"Better let go of Sita or Rama will destroy your golden city when he comes to rescue his wife," warned Hanuman.

Ravana answered, "Rama left her unguarded, I took her as the law of the jungle permits."

"Then you are just a beast, nothing more." So saying, Hanuman raised his hand and as the court watched in horror, boxed Ravana so hard that his crown fell on the floor. Hanuman grabbed the crown and threw it away.

Frothing with fury, Ravana ordered his rakshasas to set Hanuman's tail on fire.

The Burning of Lanka

The demons shoved and pushed Hanuman out and wrapped his tail with rags and ropes soaked in oil. In order to humiliate him further, he was paraded down the streets of Lanka! Then, the wicked demons set Hanuman's tail on fire. Everyone was excited at the prospect of watching the monkey with a burning tail squirm and suffer. But Hanuman had other plans.

As soon as his tail was on fire, he pushed the rakshasas away, jumped up to the roof, swung his burning tail around and set the tapestries ablaze.

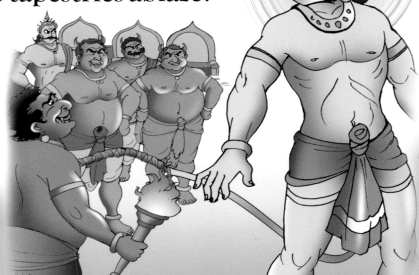

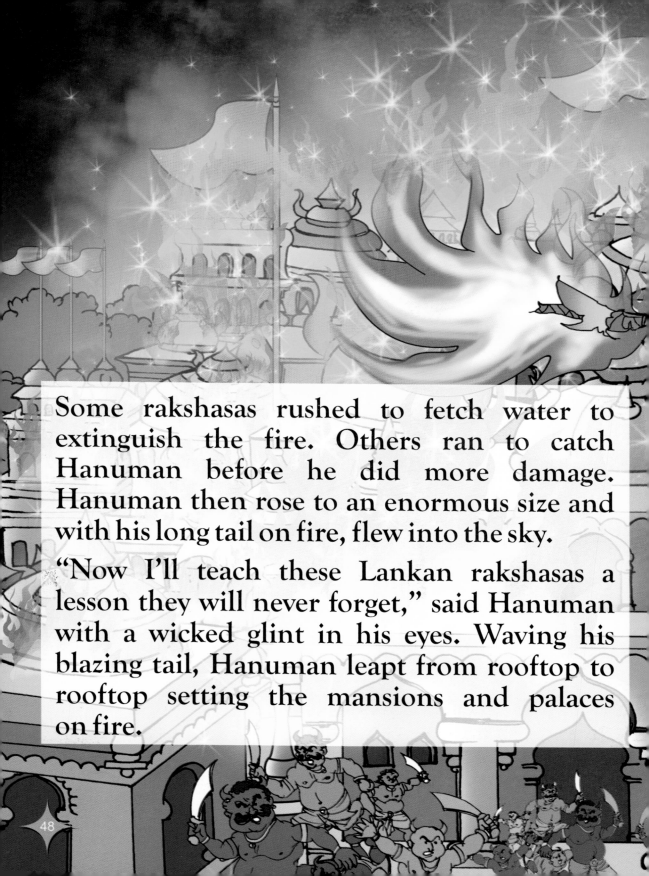

Some rakshasas rushed to fetch water to extinguish the fire. Others ran to catch Hanuman before he did more damage. Hanuman then rose to an enormous size and with his long tail on fire, flew into the sky.

"Now I'll teach these Lankan rakshasas a lesson they will never forget," said Hanuman with a wicked glint in his eyes. Waving his blazing tail, Hanuman leapt from rooftop to rooftop setting the mansions and palaces on fire.

Soon, the whole city was in flames, except Ashoka Vatika where Sita was safe.

The gold began to melt. Pillars crumbled, walls collapsed, roofs crashed. Indrajit shot an arrow into the sky forcing the clouds to shed rain. But nothing could put out the inferno.

Helpless, the rakshasas ran to the streets to save themselves.

Hanuman dipped his tail into the ocean to put out the fire. Leaving the chaotic burning city behind, he made his way back home to his waiting army and Rama.

The Bridge to Lanka

When Hanuman reached Jambudvipa, Rama rushed to him for news of Sita. As Hanuman gave him Sita's hair-pin, Rama praised him for his bravery saying, "You have given me reason to live again."

Then, the monkeys of Kishkinda led by Sugriva and Hanuman, prepared for battle with Ravana. Jambuvan joined them with a contingent of bears. Everyone followed Rama as he made his way to the coast, determined to crush the ten-headed King of Lanka.

VIBHISHANA JOINS RAMA

As Rama wondered how he could get his monkey troops across the sea, news came that a demon from Lanka was headed their way.

"Shall I shoot him down?" asked Lakshmana. "No, don't," said Hanuman. "I recognize him. It is Vibhishana, Ravana's younger brother. In Ravana's court, he was the only one who said that Sita should be allowed to return to her husband."

Ravana had banished Vibhishana from Lanka for speaking out against the abduction of Sita.

Vibhishana now sought to join forces with Rama.

PROMISE OF THE SEA-GOD

Rama pondered over the problem of getting his army across the sea to Lanka. They could neither fly like Hanuman nor swim so far. And there weren't enough trees around to build ships. There were only stones.

Desperate, Rama raised his bow and prepared to shoot a lethal arrow to force Varuna, the Sea-God, to part the waters.

"Stop," said Varuna appearing before Rama, hoping to avert this impending disaster. "The waters will not part but will keep the stones afloat, enabling you to build a bridge to Lanka," promised the Sea-God.

Pleased with the Sea-God's response, Rama lowered his bow.

Rama ordered his monkey troop to build a bridge to Lanka. A monkey named Nila designed the bridge while Hanuman oversaw it.

Before the stones were flung, Hanuman carved the name 'Rama' on the stones with his nails. "Let the rocks reverberate with the power of Rama, upholder of righteousness," announced Hanuman.

HANUMAN BRIDGES THE GAP

As the monkeys approached their destination, Ravana hurled two missiles and destroyed the two ends of the bridge. Rama and his monkey troops were left stranded on sea, unable to cross over to Lanka or return to Jambudvipa.

Before this calamity could sap the motivation of the monkeys, Hanuman thought of a plan. He increased his size and stretched himself over the gap, placing his hands on the shore of Lanka and his legs on the edge of the bridge.

The monkeys scrambled over his back and reached Ravana's island kingdom.

As Rama walked over Hanuman's back, Hanuman said, "I am blessed today for I have been touched by the feet of Rama."

Hanuman
Gets the Sacred Herb

Finally, the great war between the armies of Rama and Ravana began. During the battle, Meghnath attacked Lakshmana and rendered him unconscious.

Holding Lakshmana in his arms, Rama started crying. Hanuman could not bear to see Rama suffer thus. "How can I help?" he asked Vibhishana. Vibhishana instructed Hanuman to fetch Sushena, a skilled demon-physician, who lived in Lanka.

Hanuman immediately took the form of a bee, flew into Lanka and following directions given by Vibhishana, found the rakshasa-physician. Not wanting to risk rejection, he uprooted Sushena's house from its foundation and carried him over the walls of Lanka to where Lakshmana lay unconscious.

Sushena examined Lakshmana and said, The only herb that can act as an antidote is Sanjivani that grows on Gandhamadana, a hill that stands south of Mount Kailasa in the Himalayas," and he further added, "no one can reach there."

Who could save Lakshmana now?

"Wait!" said Hanuman as he stepped forward.

"Please do not give up hope. I will make the impossible possible!" Hanuman declared.

"But you have to get it before the setting of the moon and the rising of the sun, then I will be able to save his life," said Sushena. Hanuman flew up into the skies and raced towards the mountain that grew the precious herb. Meanwhile, King Ravana came to know of all these happenings and ordered his uncle, Kala-Nemi, a magician, to stop Hanuman from getting the life saving herb.

When Hanuman reached the Gandhamadana mountain, Kala-Nemi, disguised as a hermit, approached Hanuman and said,

"Son of Vayu, you have blessed this mountain by setting foot on it. Please bless my hermitage too by coming there and sharing a meal with us."

"I will not touch food until Lakshmana is well. But I shall certainly come to your hermitage," Hanuman said.

Before entering the hermitage, to cleanse himself, Hanuman went to bathe in a nearby lake.

In the lake lived a wicked crocodile that killed any living creature that entered its waters. As soon as Hanuman placed his foot in the water, the crocodile seized it. But Hanuman dragged the creature out and vanquished it.

From the dead body of the crocodile, a lovely apsara emerged. She folded her hands and bowed before Hanuman. By killing the crocodile, Hanuman had freed her from the curse. The Apsara informed Hanuman that the hermit was Kala-Nemi, Ravana's uncle.

Hanuman went to the hermitage. Kala-Nemi rushed to greet him. "You have honoured this little hermitage," he said in a voice full of piety.

Before he could say another word, Hanuman grabbed the hermit by his beard and raised him off the ground. "Did you think I wouldn't find out who you are?" Kala-Nemi struggled to escape but Hanuman held him in a vice-like grip.

"Your presence on this mountain will make it impure," said the Monkey-God, "go back to where you belong."

Hanuman grabbed Kala-Nemi's feet and whirled him around his head. Then he flung him as hard as he could throw. Kala-Nemi went flying through the air and landed at the foot of Ravana's throne; dead.

Fearing that Hanuman would fetch the Sanjivani in time to save Lakshmana, Ravana ordered the sun to rise and the moon to set before the appointed hour.

Hanuman saw the moon slip rapidly towards the horizon and the first light of the dawn appearing beyond the hills.

'What is this? Is the sun rising? It is only midnight?' Hanuman's mind raced.

'It must be that evil Ravana who is creating this hurdle.'

Realizing Ravana's intentions, Hanuman rushed towards the horizon.

He caught the moon between his jaws and trapped the sun in his armpit. Hanuman then dashed towards the mountain and landed on top of it.

"All the herbs are shining? Which one is Sanjivani?" Hanuman paced up and down. Time was running out. With an abrupt chortle, Hanuman decided,

"I shall carry the entire mountain to Sushena and he can choose the herb himself."

Hanuman grew in size till his head brushed against the sky. He then uprooted the hill, placed it on his palms and rushed towards Lanka. As Hanuman carried the mountain, all who saw him, were awestruck by his strength and agility.

When Hanuman arrived on the shores of Lanka and placed Gandhamadana on the ground, the monkeys roared joyously. Sushena scoured the slopes and found the Sanjivani herb. "Now all I need is the divine pestle and mortar that Ravana keeps in his inner chambers."

Hanuman immediately made his way into Ravana's palace. Unfortunately, Ravana had foreseen Sushena's need for the pestle and mortar and had placed it on a table next to his bed, determined not to let it out of his sight.

Hanuman noticed that Ravana's wife Mandodari was sleeping soundly next to Ravana and conjured a plan to distract the rakshasa-king. He slipped under Ravana's bed and tied Ravana's hair to the bedpost. He then grabbed the pestle and mortar and ran towards the door.

Ravana tried to run after Hanuman but was yanked back to his bed because his hair had been tied to the bedpost. He tried to untie the knot but failed because Hanuman had cast a spell: the knot would not be undone until Mandodari kicked Ravana on the head with her foot.

Hanuman jeered Ravana as the mighty Lord of Lanka woke his wife up, bowed his head and begged her to kick him. Hanuman then took to the air and gave Sushena the divine pestle and mortar.

Using these tools, Sushena made a paste of Sanjivani and smeared it all over Lakshmana's body. In no time, Lakshmana regained his consciousness. He stood up, ready to do battle.

Suddenly, Rama noticed that neither the sun nor the moon could be seen in the sky. "Where are they?" he asked.

"Oops," said Hanuman, opening his mouth to liberate the moon and raising his arms to free the sun.

As the moon and the sun returned to their celestial abodes, Rama and Lakshmana embraced Hanuman unable to find words to express their gratitude.

Hanuman Kills Mahiravana

Lakshmana fought with renewed vigour and enthusiasm. Finally, Lakshmana came face to face with Indrajit and after a great fight, Lakshmana's arrow severed Indrajit's neck.

Shaken by Indrajit's death, Ravana sent for his other son, Mahiravana, a powerful sorcerer.

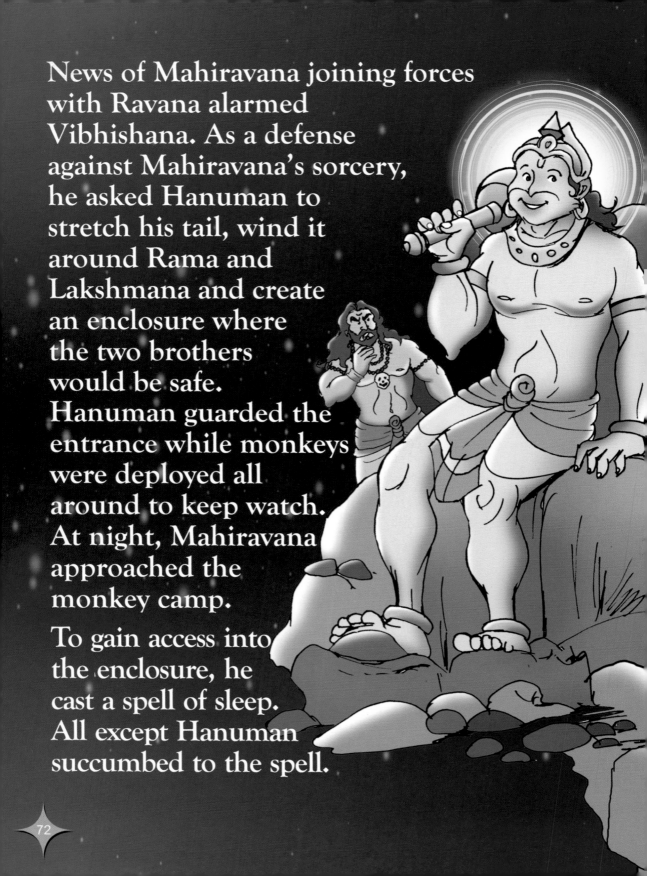

News of Mahiravana joining forces with Ravana alarmed Vibhishana. As a defense against Mahiravana's sorcery, he asked Hanuman to stretch his tail, wind it around Rama and Lakshmana and create an enclosure where the two brothers would be safe. Hanuman guarded the entrance while monkeys were deployed all around to keep watch. At night, Mahiravana approached the monkey camp.

To gain access into the enclosure, he cast a spell of sleep. All except Hanuman succumbed to the spell.

Realizing Hanuman's strength, Mahiravana decided to use trickery to gain access into the enclosure. With his magical powers, he took the form of Vibhishana and approached Hanuman. "I want to see if the brothers are comfortable," he said. Hanuman failed to recognize the imposter and let him enter.

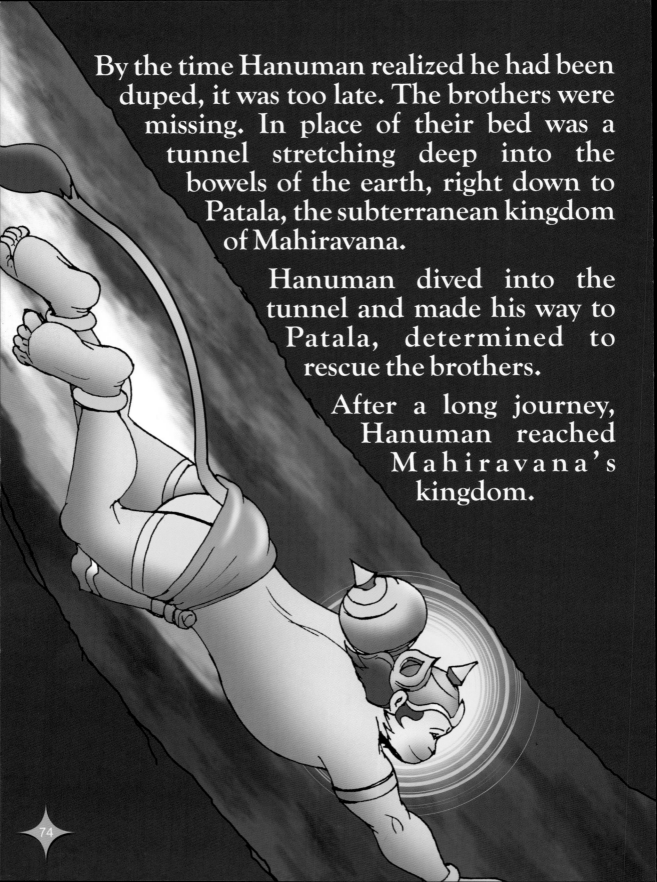

By the time Hanuman realized he had been duped, it was too late. The brothers were missing. In place of their bed was a tunnel stretching deep into the bowels of the earth, right down to Patala, the subterranean kingdom of Mahiravana.

Hanuman dived into the tunnel and made his way to Patala, determined to rescue the brothers.

After a long journey, Hanuman reached Mahiravana's kingdom.

At the gates, he was stopped by the doorkeeper who challenged him to a fight. The doorkeeper turned out to be quite a wrestler. Impressed, Hanuman enquired about his lineage.

"I am Makaradhvaja, the son of Hanuman," he said.

"Liar. I am Hanuman, Rama's devotee, sworn to celibacy. I have neither wife nor son."

Makaradhvaja fell at Hanuman's feet and revealed the secret of his birth, "As you flew across the ocean in search of Sita, a drop of your sweat fell into the sea. It was swallowed by a dolphin who as a result became pregnant and gave birth to me."

On learning of his father's mission, Makaradhvaja led Hanuman to the Kali temple where Rama and Lakshmana were being held captive. Mahiravana was planning to kill Rama and Lakshmana and offer their heads, to Goddess Kali.

Mahiravana was sharpening the sacrificial blade and chanting hymns to invoke the Goddess.

Hanuman took the form of a bee and whispered into Rama's ear, "When Mahiravana asks you to place your neck on the sacrificial block, inform him that as a member of the royal family you have never learnt to bow your head. Tell him to show you how."

Rama did as he was told and demanded that Mahiravana demonstrate how a sacrificial victim is expected to place his neck on the altar. Mahiravana bowed his head in the ritually prescribed manner. No sooner had Mahiravana done that then Hanuman seized the sacrificial blade and beheaded the sorcerer.

At dawn, the next day, the Gods assembled in the skies to witness the final battle between Rama and Ravana. Finally, on Hanuman's suggestion, Rama decided to shoot the Rudrastra. The arrow hit Ravana's navel and the king tumbled down. Thus, with Ravana's fall, Rama and Sita were once again united. Vibhishana was crowned king of Lanka. Just as he was about to leave, Rama asked Hanuman how he would like to be thanked for his services. Hanuman replied, "My Lord, let me spend the rest of my days in your service."

"So be it," said Rama. Hanuman boarded the flying chariot and followed Rama to Ayodhya.